Prescription for *Success*

Prescription for Success

Dr. Dorothy Wagner

Fawcett Columbine • New York

A Fawcett Columbine Book
Published by Ballantine Books

Library of Congress Catalog Card Number: 89-91781

ISBN: 0-449-90471-7

Manufactured in the United States of America

First Ballantine Books Edition: April 1990
10 9 8 7 6 5 4 3 2 1

Prescription for Success

You must have a dream
before you can make it
come true.

Lack of money is not a problem,
lack of motivation is.

Don't think money equates with success, many wealthy people are lonely, and miserable.

If you waste your money you can earn more, if you waste your time it is irreplaceable.

Don't focus on money. Focus on what you are doing, the money will come.

It's not the profit, but the goal that is important.

If you don't know where you are going,
you may never get there.

After careful deliberation, make up your mind then stick with it.

Successful people trust themselves.

Even the most creative people
do not always quickly attain
their goal.

Give yourself credit for how far you have come. We often take it for granted.

Others perceive you by the image you project.

Learn the art of dressing well,
otherwise you will not sell for what
you are worth.

Most of us never reach our potential because of the fear of taking chances.

Don't let your fears limit how high
you can fly!

Try to analyze what your fears are and why you fear them.

The only people who don't fail at anything are the ones who don't try anything.

It's far better to try to do something and fail than to do nothing and succeed.

Make failure a new beginning.

Get up one more time
than they knock you down.

Winners make things happen, losers wait
for the right opportunity.

Einstein credited the discovery of his theory of relativity to imagination rather than knowledge.

The world is ruled by feelings,
not reason.

Our attitude is the most important aspect of our ability to succeed.

Successful people are those who believe
that they can succeed.

What we think about we move towards.

Practice succeeding in your imagination.
See yourself where you want to be.

In your heart you must believe
your truly deserve to succeed.

Don't compare yourself to others.
Recognize your own strengths.

Don't take no for an answer!

Decca records turned down the Beatles in 1962. They said groups of guitarists were on the way out.

Countless times persistence has been the difference between success and failure.

Ignore people who say it can't be done.

Procrastination is the enemy of success.

Decision is the mastery of procrastination.

Lack of decision is one of the major causes of failure.

Not deciding is a decision.

The astronauts going to the moon were off course 90% of the time. They constantly had to adjust their course to reach their goal.

Reaching new goals sometimes means letting go of past relationships and negative situations.

There is rarely gain without pain.

What are you willing to sacrifice for success?

Discern when your most productive time is and arrange your schedule accordingly.

Don't prostitute your energies.
You must prioritize.

Keep a weekly planner. Schedule time
for recreation.

Keep paper and pencil handy at all times. Jot down any and all ideas.

Being overly organized is not a virtue.
It stifles creativity.

Persistence is a state of mind.
Make it a habit.

To the degree that we concentrate our efforts we will succeed in achieving our goal.

On my walk today, I saw a weed that had grown up through the asphalt pavement. Consider the effort!

If a weed can do it, can't you?